How to Analyze the Works of

FREDERICK DOUGLASS

by Valerie Bodden

ABDO
Publishing Company

Essential Critiques

How to Analyze the Works of

FREDERICK
DOUGLASS

by Valerie Bodden

Content Consultant: Richard W. Leeman, PhD
Professor, Department of Communication Studies
University of North Carolina–Charlotte

Credits

Published by ABDO Publishing Company, PO Box 398166, Minneapolis, MN 55439. Copyright © 2013 by Abdo Consulting Group, Inc. International copyrights reserved in all countries. No part of this book may be reproduced in any form without written permission from the publisher. The Essential Library™ is a trademark and logo of ABDO Publishing Company

Printed in the United States of America,
North Mankato, Minnesota
102012
012013

 THIS BOOK CONTAINS AT LEAST 10% RECYCLED MATERIALS.

Editor: Angela Wiechmann
Series Designer: Marie Tupy

Cataloging-in-Publication Data
Bodden, Valerie.
 How to analyze the works of Frederick Douglass / Valerie Bodden.
  p. cm. -- (Essential critiques)
Includes bibliographical references and index.
ISBN 978-1-61783-644-2
1. Douglass, Frederick--1818-1895--Criticism and interpretation--Juvenile literature. 2. Abolitionists--United States--Juvenile literature. 3. African American abolitionists--Juvenile literature. 4. Slaves--United States--Juvenile literature. I. Title.
973.8--dc14

2012946238

Table of Contents

1

Introduction to Critiques

What Is Critical Theory?

What do you usually do when you read a book or essay or listen to a speech? You probably absorb the specific language style of the work. You also consider the point the speaker or writer is trying to convey. Yet these are only a few of many possible ways of understanding and appreciating a speech or piece of writing. What if you are interested in delving more deeply? You might want to learn more about the writer or speaker and how his or her personal background is reflected in the work. Or you might want to examine what the work says about society—how it depicts the roles of women and minorities, for example. If so, you have entered the realm of critical theory.

Critical theory helps you learn how art, literature, music, theater, film, speeches, and other endeavors either support or challenge the way society behaves. Critical theory is the evaluation and interpretation of a work using different philosophies, or schools of thought. Critical theory can be used to understand all types of cultural works.

There are many different critical theories. Each theory asks you to look at the work from a different perspective. Some theories address social issues, while others focus on the writer's or speaker's life or the time period in which the work was written. For example, the critical theory that asks how an author's life affected the work is called biographical criticism. Other common schools of criticism include historical criticism, feminist criticism, psychological criticism, and New Criticism, which examines a work solely within the context of the work itself.

What Is the Purpose of Critical Theory?

Critical theory can open your mind to new ways of thinking. It can help you evaluate a piece of writing or speech from a new perspective, directing your attention to issues and messages you may not otherwise recognize in a work. For example, applying feminist criticism to an essay may make you aware of female stereotypes perpetuated in the work. Applying a critical theory to a speech helps you learn about the person who gave it or the society that heard it. You can also explore how the work is perceived by current cultures.

How Do You Apply Critical Theory?

You conduct a critique when you use a critical theory to examine and question a work. The theory you choose is a lens through which you can view the work, or a springboard for asking questions about the work. Applying a critical theory helps you think critically about the work. You are free to question the work and make assertions about it. If you choose to examine an essay using biographical criticism, for example, you want to know how the writer's personal background or education inspired or shaped the work. You could explore why the writer was drawn to the subject. For instance, are there any parallels between points raised in the essay and details from the writer's life?

Forming a Thesis

Ask your question and find answers in the work or other related materials. Then you can create a thesis. The thesis is the key point in your critique. It is your argument about the work based on the tenets, or beliefs, of the theory you are using. For example, if you are using biographical criticism to ask how the writer's life inspired the work, your thesis could be worded as follows: Writer Teng Xiong, raised in refugee camps in Southeast Asia, drew upon her experiences to write the essay "No Home for Me."

How to Make
a Thesis Statement

In a critique, a thesis statement typically appears at the end of the introductory paragraph. It is usually only one sentence long and states the author's main idea.

Providing Evidence

Once you have formed a thesis, you must provide evidence to support it. Evidence might take the form of examples and quotations from the work itself—such as excerpts from an essay. Articles about the essay or personal interviews with the writer might also support your ideas. You may wish to address what other critics have written about the work. Quotes from these individuals may help support your claim. If you find any quotes or examples that contradict your thesis, you will need to create an argument against them. For instance: <u>Many critics have pointed to the essay "No Home for Me" as detailing only the powerless circumstances Xiong faced. However, in the paragraphs focused on her emigration to the United States, Xiong clearly depicts herself as someone who can shape her own future.</u>

> **How to Support a Thesis Statement**
>
> A critique should include several arguments. Arguments support a thesis claim. An argument is one or two sentences long and is supported by evidence from the work being discussed.
>
> Organize the arguments into paragraphs. These paragraphs make up the body of the critique.

In This Book

In this book, you will read summaries of famous works by Frederick Douglass, each followed by a critique. Each critique will use one theory and apply it to one work. Critical thinking sections will give you a chance to consider other theses and questions about the work. Did you agree with the author's application of the theory? What other questions are raised by the thesis and its arguments? You can also find out what other critics think about each work. Then, in the You Critique It section in the final pages of this book, you will have an opportunity to create your own critique.

> **Look for the Guides**
>
> Throughout the chapters that analyze the works, thesis statements have been highlighted. The box next to the thesis helps explain what questions are being raised about the work. Supporting arguments have been underlined. The boxes next to the arguments help explain how these points support the thesis. Look for these guides throughout each critique.

Frederick changed his last name to Douglass after he escaped from slavery to help him evade slave catchers.

2

A Closer Look at Frederick Douglass

After spending the first 20 years of his life in slavery, Frederick Douglass ran away to find freedom in the northern half of the United States. But Douglass was not content with achieving only his own freedom. From the time he escaped until his death 57 years later, Douglass spoke out for the freedom and equal treatment of his fellow African Americans as an orator, editor, and diplomat.

A Young Slave

Frederick Douglass was born Frederick Augustus Washington Bailey in Tuckahoe, Maryland, a region in Talbot County, in February 1818. His mother, Harriet Bailey, was also a slave. She was hired out to a different farm while Frederick was a baby, and he saw her only a few times in his life. Frederick never knew his white father's identity for certain, but he was aware of rumors that his slave owner was also his father.

Frederick lived with his grandmother, Betsy Bailey, in a cabin in the woods until he was six years old. Then, his grandmother was required to bring him to the estate of his slave owner, Aaron Anthony, where he remained for two years.

At the age of eight, Frederick was sent to live with Hugh Auld (the brother of Anthony's son-in-law) and his wife, Sophia, in Baltimore, Maryland. Sophia treated Frederick well and even began teaching him to read. The determined boy eventually taught himself to read and write.

The Hard Life

In 1833, at the age of 15, Frederick was sent to Saint Michaels, Maryland, where Thomas Auld, his new owner, lived. Frederick wasn't much use to Auld, however, so in 1834, the owner sent his slave to the farm of Edward Covey, a notorious "slave breaker."

In 1835, Frederick was hired out to another local farmer named William Freeland. Frederick and four other slaves planned an escape, but before they could carry it out, they were discovered. Afterward, Frederick was sent back to Hugh Auld in Baltimore. This time, Auld hired him out as a caulker in a shipyard.

Finding Freedom

On September 3, 1838, the 20-year-old Douglass dressed as a sailor and made his escape via train, ferry, and steamboat. His destination was New York City. Immediately after arriving, Douglass sent a letter to Anna Murray, a free black woman he had begun to court in Baltimore. Murray joined Douglass in New York, and on September 15, the two were married.

Douglass and his bride made their first home in New Bedford, Massachusetts. There, Douglass took a number of odd jobs before finding work on a wharf. The Douglasses also began their family in New Bedford, with the birth of daughter Rosetta on June 24, 1839, and son Lewis Henry on October 9, 1840.

Abolitionist Beginnings

Douglass had first heard the word *abolitionist* as a child. Now, with his own escape complete, he joined the ranks of those calling for the abolition of slavery in the United States. Beginning in 1839, he spoke out at small meetings in New Bedford. Then, on August 16, 1841, Douglass was asked to make a speech at the summer meeting of the Massachusetts Anti-Slavery Society. Afterward, the society hired him as a speaker.

Douglass moved his family to Lynn, Massachusetts, and began traveling tirelessly, delivering more than 100 speeches a year. Douglass was a powerful speaker. His speeches were so well delivered, in fact, some opponents began questioning whether Douglass had actually been a slave. In order to prove his experiences were true, Douglass decided to write an autobiography. *Narrative of the Life of Frederick Douglass, An American Slave, Written by Himself* was published in 1845.

Douglass's autobiography was a huge success. But its popularity also made remaining in the United States dangerous for Douglass, who could be captured and returned to Thomas Auld. Douglass sailed for Great Britain, leaving behind his family, which now included two more children—Frederick Jr., born in 1842, and Charles Remond, born in 1844.

Freedom

When Douglass returned to the United States in 1847, he was a free man. His British supporters had raised $1,250 (approximately $35,000 today) to buy his freedom. Their money also enabled Douglass to establish a weekly abolitionist newspaper called *North Star* in Rochester, New York, where he moved his family to in 1847. In 1849, Douglass's fifth child, Annie, was born.

In 1855, Douglass published another autobiography, titled *My Bondage and My Freedom*. It recounts not only the horrors he suffered as a slave but also the prejudice he faced in the North since his escape.

In October 1859, abolitionist John Brown attempted to raid the federal arsenal at Harpers Ferry, Virginia. Although Brown had invited Douglass to participate, Douglass declined. Even so, after the raid, a note from Douglass was found in Brown's possession. In order to avoid arrest, Douglass quickly escaped to Canada and then continued on to England for an already planned lecture tour. Four months later, on March 13, 1860, Douglass's youngest daughter died, and he set off for home to be with his family.

Civil War

In March 1861, Abraham Lincoln became president of the United States. By the next month, the country was embroiled in civil war. In 1861, Douglass began calling for the United States to enlist black men in the war effort for the Union. Two years later, the governor of Massachusetts sought black men to serve in the Fifty-fourth Massachusetts Volunteers. Douglass aided in recruitment efforts, signing up two of his sons, along with more than 100 others. That same year, Douglass was also invited to meet with President Lincoln to discuss the treatment of black soldiers in the Union army.

The Civil War ended in 1865, and the Thirteenth Amendment to the US Constitution brought emancipation of the slaves. Douglass could again be found on the lecture trail. Now, rather than calling for an end to slavery, Douglass spoke out in favor of equal treatment for blacks, including the right to vote.

On to Washington

In 1871, President Ulysses S. Grant appointed Douglass to serve as secretary to the Santo

Domingo Commission. The commission's task was to explore the possibility of annexing the island of the Dominican Republic, although the proposal went nowhere.

In 1863, Douglass met with President Lincoln to discuss the treatment of black soldiers.

While Douglass was in Washington DC in June 1872, his house in Rochester burned down. Douglass now moved his family to Washington, where, in March 1874, he became president of the Freedman's Savings and Trust Company. Only four months later, the bank—which had already been in bad financial shape when Douglass took over—failed.

Moving on from the bank disaster, Douglass accepted a position as marshal of the District of Columbia in 1877. In 1881, he was given a new position as recorder of deeds for the District of Columbia. That year, he also published a final autobiography, *The Life and Times of Frederick Douglass*. He later updated it in 1892.

On August 4, 1882, Douglass's wife Anna died of a stroke. A year and a half later, on January 24, 1884, Douglass married Helen Pitts, a white woman who had worked as a clerk in his office. Many black Americans decried the marriage, as they felt Douglass was rejecting his own people by marrying a white woman.

In 1889, President Benjamin Harrison appointed Douglass minister to Haiti. Douglass and his wife arrived in the country in October. However, Douglass faced some criticism after failing to negotiate for the lease of a naval station on the island, and he resigned his post on July 30, 1891.

Even after he returned to the United States, Douglass remained tied to Haiti. He served as commissioner of the Republic of Haiti pavilion at the World's Columbian Exposition, held in Chicago, Illinois, in 1893.

Honored in Death

On February 20, 1895, Frederick Douglass died of a heart attack. After memorial services in Washington, which were attended by thousands of black schoolchildren as well as US senators and a Supreme Court justice, his body was taken to Rochester. There, another memorial was held before Douglass's body was buried in the local cemetery.

Today Douglass's legacy lives on. It has inspired countless civil rights workers over the years. Because he rose above his life of slavery and used his masterful writing and speaking to challenge society, Douglass is still regarded as one of the most influential champions of African-American rights.

Essential Critiques

Douglass spent his earliest years with his grandmother in a small slave cabin such as this.

3

An Overview of *Narrative of the Life of Frederick Douglass*

The first of Douglass's three autobiographies—*Narrative of the Life of Frederick Douglass, A Slave, Written by Himself*—was published in 1845. In telling the story of his life, Douglass offered not only an emotional rendering of the conditions experienced by slaves but also a compelling antislavery argument. The book was popular with readers of Douglass's day, selling 30,000 copies in the first five years after its publication, and students and scholars today still study it.[1]

Born into Slavery

Douglass begins the account of his life with his birth in Tuckahoe, an area in Talbot County, Maryland. He gives few details about his birth, because he knows little about it. He doesn't even know his own birthday, a fact that made him unhappy during childhood: "The white children could tell their ages. I could not tell why I ought to be deprived of the same privilege."[2]

Young Frederick was raised by his grandmother in a small cabin and rarely saw his mother, who died when he was approximately seven or eight years old. Frederick never knew who his father was or even if he was his white slave owner. And he was not the only slave to suffer this uncertainty. Douglass says many slaves were products of their owners' affairs with slave women. In some cases, the slave owners had to sell these slaves—their own children—in order to appease their white wives, who disapproved of the affairs.

Witnessing Slavery's Cruelty

After spending his early years with his grandmother at another site on the large plantation, Frederick was sent to live in the home of his first owner, Aaron Anthony. Anthony was an unkind owner who took cruel joy in whipping his slaves, including Frederick's aunt, who was forced to stand naked from the waist up, with her arms tied above her head, until her back was covered in blood.

Even as he witnessed such cruelties, however, young Frederick experienced little of them himself. He was still too young to work in the field and was rarely whipped. He did, however, frequently experience hunger and cold. He recalls hearing his fellow slaves sing songs that he, as a young child, did not yet realize expressed supreme anguish.

City Life

When he was seven or eight years old, Frederick was sent to Baltimore to live with Hugh and Sophia Auld. When he arrived at the Aulds', he saw "what I had never seen before; it was a white face beaming with the most kindly emotions; it was the face of my new mistress, Sophia Auld."[3]

Sophia's kindness extended to teaching Frederick to read. But soon after she had begun, her husband told her she must stop; it was not fitting or even legal to teach a slave to read. Despite the fact that he no longer had his mistress teaching him, Frederick was determined to learn how to read. He made friends with the white children in the street, many of whom were hungry and would teach him in return for bread. He also copied the letters he saw on timbers at the shipyard and in the Aulds' son's used spelling books. Once he had learned to read, however, Frederick became more aware of his enslavement, and at times he despaired, thinking he would never be free.

Fighting Back

After living in Baltimore for approximately five years with Hugh and Sophia Auld, Aaron Anthony, Frederick's owner, died. All of Anthony's slaves were called back to the plantation where Frederick had been raised. As Anthony's children divided their father's estate, Frederick and the other slaves were inhumanely "valued" with livestock and other property.[4] Frederick was relieved that Anthony's children decided to send him back to Hugh Auld's home in Baltimore.

When Frederick was approximately 12 or 13 years old, Thomas Auld called him back to serve him in Saint Michaels. Unlike his brother, Hugh, Thomas did not provide enough food for Frederick. Even after Thomas experienced a conversion to Christianity, he remained a cruel man, despite Frederick's hopes that religion would change him.

After nine months, Thomas decided city life had made Frederick almost unfit to be a slave.

So he sent the boy to Edward Covey "to be broken."[5] Frederick was put to work as a field hand, and within a week, Covey had given Frederick a severe whipping. Nearly weekly whippings followed, and in a short time, Covey had succeeded in breaking Frederick's spirits. "My natural elasticity was crushed, my intellect languished, the disposition to read departed, the cheerful spark that lingered about my eye died," he writes of that time.[6] Living on the Chesapeake Bay, Frederick envied the ships he saw sailing out to sea, for they were "freedom's swift-winged angels, that fly round the world."[7]

After more than six months at Covey's, Frederick and three other slaves were working with harvested wheat when Frederick fell ill and fainted. When Covey told him to get up, Frederick couldn't, so Covey kicked him and struck him with a heavy piece of wood. Having enough of such treatment, Frederick decided to complain to his owner. With his head wound still bleeding, he set off through the woods for the seven-mile (11.3 km) walk to Thomas Auld's house. After five hours, he finally reached Auld, but his owner offered no help and sent Frederick back to Covey.

As he was returning, Frederick came upon Sandy Jenkins, another slave. Jenkins gave Frederick a certain root, telling him if he carried it, it would keep him safe from Covey's whippings. A few days after his return to Covey's farm, Frederick was caring for the horses when Covey attempted to tie him up. Frederick, however, managed to get out of Covey's grasp and began fighting back. After two hours of fighting, Covey finally let Frederick go and never beat him again. Douglass marks the fight with Covey as a pivotal moment in his life, his courage perhaps inspired by the root. It renewed his desire for freedom.

Escape Attempt

After a year in Covey's service, Frederick was sent to William Freeland, a much kinder slave owner. Frederick made friends with two of the other slaves at Freeland's and even began to teach them to read. Soon, neighboring slaves wanted to learn, too, so Frederick held a Sabbath school. He found teaching his fellow slaves one of the few delights of his time in slavery.

As 1835 began, Frederick decided to plan his escape. Not willing to see his friends remain in

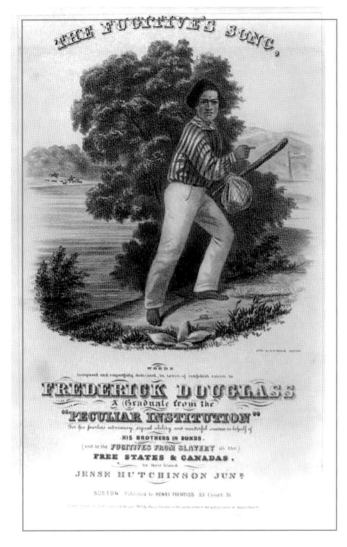

"The Fugitive's Song" was a piece of music inspired by Douglass's escape from slavery.

slavery, he included them in his plans as well. On the Saturday night before Easter, Frederick and four others intended to take a canoe up the Chesapeake Bay approximately 80 miles (127 km) and then walk, following the North Star, until they reached the free North. That morning, however, their plan was discovered. After spending a week in jail, Frederick was sent once again to Hugh Auld in Baltimore.

This time, Auld hired out Frederick to a shipbuilder, where he learned to be a ship caulker. His skill earned him up to nine dollars a week, all of which he had to turn over to Auld. Even after he began contracting for his own work—and renting his own place—he had to pay Auld most of his wages. He was grimly aware of the injustice.

Escape

Now approximately 20 years old, Douglass arranged with some friends to go to a camp meeting outside the city. He was unable to get his weekly wages to Auld before he left town but made sure to do so immediately upon returning. This was not good enough for his owner, however, who demanded Douglass return to live at the Auld home.

At this, Douglass decided again to make his escape. On September 3, 1838, he left Baltimore— and his life of slavery. In *Narrative*, Frederick chose not to recount the specific details of his escape so other slaves could safely use the same route after

the book's publication. When Douglass arrived in
New York, he was taken in by David Ruggles, a
New Yorker who helped fugitive slaves find safety.
Soon, Douglass's intended wife, Anna, arrived, and
the two were married. Immediately afterward, they
left New York for New Bedford, Massachusetts.

Abolitionist Beginnings

In New Bedford, Douglass was impressed
by the wealth he saw. He was gratified, too, by
the conditions in which the black people of the
city lived.

Within three days of his arrival in New Bedford,
Douglass attained work filling a ship with oil.
Although it was a hard, dirty job, he labored
joyfully, knowing he was working for himself and
his new wife—and not for a white slave owner.

Douglass began attending antislavery meetings,
and on August 11, 1841, he was persuaded to
speak at a convention in Nantucket. Although he
was reluctant to take on the burden of sharing
his experiences in slavery, he rose to speak. That
occasion marked the beginning of his career
"pleading the cause of my brethren."[8] The success
of his work would speak for itself.

Frederick Douglass's autobiography depicts slavery as an immoral institution.

How to Apply Moralist Criticism to *Narrative of the Life of Frederick Douglass*

No. 2

What Is Moralist Criticism?

The word *moral* refers to the principles determining what is right or wrong. Moralist criticism, therefore, involves analyzing a work in terms of what it presents as the right or wrong way of living. Moralist critics may examine whether an individual character's actions are in line with the morals a society has established. Or it may look at whether an entire society's belief system is moral or immoral.

Applying Moralist Criticism to *Narrative of the Life of Frederick Douglass*

By the time Douglass wrote the autobiography *Narrative of the Life of Frederick Douglass*, slavery had existed in America for more than

200 years. For some, it was an unquestioned way of life. But others—most notably the abolitionists of the North—were beginning to question the morality of the institution. Among them was runaway slave Douglass.

In *Narrative*, Douglass reveals the immorality of a system that robs slaves of their humanity by taking away their physical, spiritual, and intellectual freedoms.

Most obviously, slavery strips black men and women of their physical freedom. Slaves have no say in who will own them or where they will live or work. For example, Douglass describes how he is called back from Baltimore to the plantation so he can be valued with the other property when his owner dies. "A single word from the white men was enough—against all our wishes, prayers, and entreaties—to sunder [separate] forever

Thesis Statement

The author presents the thesis at the end of this paragraph: "In *Narrative*, Douglass reveals the immorality of a system that robs slaves of their humanity by taking away their physical, spiritual, and intellectual freedoms." The author examines how slavery takes away slaves' freedoms, an immoral act that leaves them feeling less than human.

Argument One

This is the first argument: "Most obviously, slavery strips black men and women of their physical freedom." In this paragraph, the author explores how slavery denies slaves the ability to decide where to live or how to care for their bodies.

the dearest friends, dearest kindred, and strongest ties known to human beings."[1] In addition, slaves have no ability—or even right—to take care of their bodies. Douglass writes how he often experiences hunger and cold and frequently witnesses—and is a victim of—harsh beatings. Slaves are forced to do bodily work in their owners' fields or homes. Even when hired out to work for others, the slaves must turn over every cent of their wages to their owners. When Douglass is hired out, he must give the money to Hugh Auld "not because he earned it, . . . not because I owed it to him, . . . but solely because he had the power to compel me to give it up."[2]

With no right to control their bodies, Douglass shows how slaves also lose their spiritual freedom. He points out that slave songs are "the prayer and complaint of souls boiling over with the bitterest anguish."[3] Douglass, too, feels anguish when he contemplates his situation in slavery: "This everlasting thinking of my condition . . . tormented me. There was no getting rid of it. It was pressed upon me by

> **Argument Two**
> The author next shows how slavery affects the spiritual well-being of its victims. Argument two is: "With no right to control their bodies, Douglass shows how slaves also lose their spiritual freedom."

every object within sight or hearing, animate or inanimate."[4] By the time he has sustained six months of beatings by Covey, Douglass finds he is "broken in body, soul, and spirit."[5] He no longer has any desire to read or even think, and his naturally cheerful attitude disappears.

In Douglass's view, the greatest moral outrage of slavery is denying slaves' intellectual freedom by preventing them from acquiring even the most rudimentary education. Douglass's first hint of the power of education comes when Hugh Auld prevents his wife from teaching the young slave to read. Auld says teaching a slave to read would spoil him and "forever unfit him to be a slave."[6] Douglass states that when he hears this, he realizes he has discovered "the white man's power to enslave the black man."[7] If a slave remains uneducated, he is unlikely to question his lot in life. "I have found that, to make a contented slave, it is necessary to make a thoughtless one," Douglass writes.[8] Being

Argument Three

In this paragraph, the author looks at how slavery denies slaves the right to learn and educate themselves about their inequities. The third argument is: "In Douglass's view, the greatest moral outrage of slavery is denying slaves' intellectual freedom by preventing them from acquiring even the most rudimentary education."

In 1943, workers helped build the Liberty ship *Frederick Douglass* in a Baltimore shipyard similar to the one where Douglass worked as a slave.

denied intellectual freedom prevents a slave from seeking any type of freedom.

The loss of their physical, spiritual, and intellectual freedoms strips slaves of their humanity and renders them little more than animals. Like animals, slaves are left with little sense of a personal identity. Most slaves "know as little of their ages as horses know of theirs."[9] Nor do

> **Argument Four**
> This is the final argument: "The loss of their physical, spiritual, and intellectual freedoms strips slaves of their humanity and renders them little more than animals." In this paragraph, the author explores how being denied these forms of freedom takes away slaves' humanity.

many slaves know their fathers' identities. Slaves are treated like animals by their owners as well. When the slaves have to be valued, they are ranked together with the livestock: "There were horses and men, cattle and women, pigs and children, all holding the same rank in the scale of being."[10] As they are treated like animals, slaves come to see themselves as animals. After his experiences with Covey, Douglass feels his humanity is completely gone: "The dark night of slavery closed in upon me; and behold a man transformed into a brute!"[11]

Conclusion

In the conclusion, the author restates the thesis and shows how Douglass regains his humanity by regaining his physical, spiritual, and intellectual freedoms.

In the end, Douglass shows that by regaining his physical, spiritual, and intellectual freedom, he is able to regain his humanity. He gains his intellectual freedom by learning to read. Douglass finds his spirit is freed after he fights with Covey. After this, he may be a "slave in form," but he would never again be a "slave in fact."[12] With his escape to the North, Douglass regains his physical freedom, and the culminating piece of his humanity is restored.

Thinking Critically about *Narrative of the Life of Frederick Douglass*

Now it is your turn to assess the critique. Consider these questions:

1. The author argues that slavery was immoral because it deprived slaves of their physical, spiritual, and intellectual freedoms. Are there other reasons why slavery was immoral?

2. Which argument do you think is the strongest? Which is the weakest? Why?

3. The author concludes that Douglass cannot regain his humanity until he regains his physical, spiritual, and intellectual freedoms. Do you agree? Were there other steps to regaining his humanity?

Other Approaches

Narrative of the Life of Frederick Douglass is an autobiography of someone who lived under the immoral institution of slavery. Therefore, the essay above is just one way to apply moralist criticism to the work. There are many different perspectives a moralist critic could apply. For example, another approach might involve examining Douglass's criticism of hypocritical Christian slave owners. In yet another approach, a critic might reveal how the wrongs of slavery degrade slave owners.

Hypocritical Religion

Throughout *Narrative*, Douglass focuses on the hypocrisy of the Christian religion in the United States for allowing—and even supporting—the institution of slavery. He asserts that the cruelest slave owners are "good" Christians within their community. A thesis for a critique that takes this approach might be: Douglass criticizes slave owners for proclaiming to belong to a Christian religion of morality and love while they commit inhuman acts within the system of slavery. As evidence of this thesis, one supporting argument might focus on Thomas Auld, who becomes even crueler after converting to Christianity.

Morally Degrading

Narrative shows not only how slavery affects slaves but also how it reduces the morality of even once-kind slave owners. A thesis statement supporting a critique with this approach might be: Douglass reveals how the system of slavery affects slave owners, leading to their moral degradation. In a supporting argument of this thesis, a moralist critic may discuss the moral decay of Sophia Auld, who had never owned a slave before young Douglass came to live with her family. Once kind enough to teach Douglass how to read, the effects of slavery eventually make her cruel.

Real-life hero Madison Washington led a mutiny on a slave ship and sailed his fellow slaves to freedom.

5

An Overview of "The Heroic Slave"

Published in 1852, "The Heroic Slave" is Douglass's only work of fiction. The novella is based on an 1841 revolt led by a slave named Madison Washington aboard the slave ship *Creole*. The ship was bound for the New Orleans, Louisiana, slave market, but Washington sailed it to Nassau, in the Bahamas, where the slaves were set free. In "The Heroic Slave," Douglass invents a backstory for Washington's revolt.

A New Hero

"The Heroic Slave" begins with a statement about the heroes of the past who have hailed from Virginia, including George Washington and Thomas Jefferson. But one of the state's greatest heroes "holds now no higher place in the records of that grand old Commonwealth than is held by a horse or an ox."[1] Few records of this hero's deeds exist, and thus all that can be presented of his story is "marks, traces, possibles, and probabilities."[2]

Encounter in the Woods

The action of the story begins as Mr. Listwell, a white traveler from the North, rides through the Virginia countryside in 1835. Hearing a voice, Listwell follows the sound into a pine forest. There, he listens as a slave (whose name we soon learn is Madison) pours out the torment of his soul to the silent forest. The slave is handsome and strong, and his words are eloquent. He says life to him is "aimless and worthless, and worse than worthless."[3] The slave then rebukes himself for not fighting off the fetters of slavery. He resolves to be free.

The Runaway

Five years later, Listwell and his wife are inside their Ohio home on a cold winter night when there is a knock on the door. Opening it, Listwell is surprised to recognize the slave from the woods. Madison, of course, does not know Listwell but has simply stopped at the home in hopes of finding shelter. Listwell invites him inside and provides him with the best room in the house. Mrs. Listwell prepares a meal for the weary slave, who is unsure how to react, for it is the first time he has ever "met so humane and friendly a greeting at the hands of persons whose color was unlike his own."[4]

After supper, Listwell reveals to Madison that he had seen him in the Virginia woods five years earlier. Madison explains he had fled to those woods after being tied to the limb of a tree and whipped 40 times on his naked back. Although Madison had started out for the North, he never made it past his owner's land because clouds obscured his guide, the North Star. He kept himself hidden, even from his fellow slaves, whom he saw in their quarters. Finding himself back where he started after one week, he decided to live in the woods nearby so he would not have to leave his wife; she remained in service to the slave owner but came out to meet Madison at least once a week.

For five years, Madison remained in the woods, but then a fire burned down the entire forest. Madison left once again for the North. Two weeks before arriving at the Listwells', he met a slave in the forest. He gave the slave his only dollar, asking him to bring back some cheese and crackers. When the man returned, however, 14 armed white men were with him. Madison did not think the slave had betrayed him, but instead believed the slave had been forced to explain how he had gotten the dollar. When the white men couldn't find Madison in the forest, they accused the other slave of stealing the money. Stripping his shirt, they gave him 39 lashes.

Listwell contemplates how to get the escaped slave out of the country and into Canada. The next evening, after giving Madison new clothing and money, Listwell takes him to Cleveland. There, Madison boards a boat to Canada. A few days later, Listwell receives a letter from Madison, stating he is now safe and free.

Recaptured

A year after Madison's successful escape to Canada, Listwell is once again in Virginia. He finds 130 slaves in chains outside the tavern, on their way to a slave sale in Richmond. As he ponders their sad situation, Listwell is startled to recognize one of them: it is Madison Washington.

Madison reveals to Listwell how he has come to be in chains again. Shortly after arriving in

Canada, Madison resolved to risk his own freedom to save his wife. He journeyed back to his old slave owner's plantation, where he raised a ladder to his wife's window. Frightened by the noise outside her window, his wife screamed and fainted. By the time the two reached the ground, the owner and his sons were after them. Madison's wife was shot and killed, and he himself fought the men as long as he could before being overpowered. He was chained up for three days, during which time other owners brought their slaves to see him, "as proof of the completeness of [the owners'] power, and of the impossibility of slaves getting away."[5] Once his wounds healed, Madison was given 60 lashes on his back and then sold to a slave trader. He is now part of a slave gang bound for the New Orleans slave market.

After listening to Madison's story, Listwell follows at a distance as the slaves continue their march to Richmond, where they will board a ship for New Orleans. Once he arrives in Richmond, he visits a hardware store to purchase three steel files. Then, he silently slips the files into Madison's pocket.

Like Madison in "The Heroic Slave," these runaway slaves were captured in the North and returned to the South and their life of slavery.

Mutiny

Two months after Madison sails from Richmond, a group of men meets at a Richmond coffeehouse. They discuss a mutiny aboard the *Creole*, the slave ship on which Madison sailed. One of them, Tom Grant, had been first mate on that ship.

Another man, Jack Williams, demands to know how the slaves, who had been chained together below deck, could have gotten free and taken control of the ship. Grant explains that Madison must have brought three files onboard, with which he had cut his own chains, as well as those of 18 other slaves. Around twilight on the ninth day out from Richmond, Grant suddenly heard a pistol fire and looked up to see 19 slaves on deck. As Grant tried to draw his knife from his pocket, he was knocked to the deck and fell unconscious. When he came to a few minutes later, he found the white sailors up the ship's rigging, afraid to come down. The ship's captain and the slave owner lay dying on the deck, while Madison stood at the ship's helm.

Madison said, "God is my witness that LIBERTY, not *malice*, is the motive for this night's work. . . . We have done that which you applaud your fathers for doing, and if we are murderers, *so were they*."[6]

Madison then ordered the white sailors to bring the ship to port in Nassau. There, a company of black soldiers was sent aboard to protect the property. Although told that the laws of the United States made the slaves "as much property as the barrels of flour in the hold," the soldiers allowed the slaves to walk past them off the ship and into freedom.[7]

Douglass presents his hero in an appealing way to nineteenth-century white readers, even comparing him to the Greek hero Hercules.

How to Apply Racial Criticism to "The Heroic Slave"

What Is Racial Criticism?

Racial criticism involves exploring the ways in which a work presents a certain race. Racial critics may examine what it means to belong to a certain race or how a person's race informs his or her experiences. They may explore how a work upholds or tears down racial stereotypes. Or they may examine the interaction between people of different races.

Applying Racial Criticism to "The Heroic Slave"

In "The Heroic Slave," Douglass presents the story of the black hero Madison Washington. But because his story is intended for nineteenth-century white readers, Douglass does not focus on the

Thesis Statement

This is the thesis: "To make Madison appeal to his readers, Douglass portrays him according to a white ideal, removes him from the presence of other blacks, and shows his influence on white characters." In the body of the critique, the author gives examples of how Madison appeals to white readers.

Argument One

The first argument focuses on how Madison is presented with stereotypically white characteristics: "Madison's physical appearance, speech, and background appeal to a white audience."

hero's identity as an African American. To make Madison appeal to his readers, Douglass portrays him according to a white ideal, removes him from the presence of other blacks, and shows his influence on white characters.

Madison's physical appearance, speech, and background appeal to a white audience. In an 1849 speech about the real-life hero, Douglass described Madison as having a "woolly head, high cheek bones, protruding lip, distended nostril, and retreating forehead."[1] In "The Heroic Slave," however, Douglass ignores these stereotypically African-American features. Instead, he highlights Madison's other stereotypically African-American traits—such as his strength and dark complexion—in ways that are attractive to Douglass's white audience. For example, he describes Madison's strength as "Herculean," adding that he is "tall, symmetrical, round, and strong" and that his arms are "like polished iron."[2] For Madison's complexion, Douglas writes that his brow is "as dark and glossy as a raven's wing," and that his face is "black, but comely."[3]

In addition to his appearance, Madison's intelligence and behavior sets him apart from other slaves. Instead of the slave dialect common to the South, Madison uses the same educated language as the book's white readers. When Listwell first hears Madison in the forest, he is entranced by the slave's "eloquent utterances."[4] Douglass focuses on Madison as a descendent, so to say, of the white heroes of Virginia, such as Thomas Jefferson and Patrick Henry. He, like them, is a leader and a fighter for liberty.

<u>Throughout the novella, Madison spends few scenes in the presence of other blacks, and the ones he does encounter are either objects of contempt or are almost his undoing.</u> After attempting to escape but finding himself still on his slave owner's land, Madison peers

Argument Two

This is the second argument: "Throughout the novella, Madison spends few scenes in the presence of other blacks, and the ones he does encounter are either objects of contempt or are almost his undoing." In this paragraph, the author discusses what happens when Madison meets other black characters.

Madison secretly observes fellow slaves in their cabins, such as these on a Georgia plantation.

in upon the slave quarters. He is disgusted by the slaves who sit by the fire, "merrily passing away the time, as though their hearts knew no sorrow."[5] Such merriment, he says, shows "cowardly acquiescence in their own degradation."[6] Later, the slave in the woods whom Madison asks to purchase food for him leads a group of white men into the forest, where they mount a search for Madison and narrowly miss discovering him. And when he goes back to rescue his wife from the plantation, her scream gives away their escape and leads to Madison's recapture.

Douglass most often shows Madison in the presence of white characters, from whose point of view readers see the story. The first part of the book comes to readers largely from the point of view of Listwell, who first encounters Madison in the forest pouring out the torments of his soul. Although the two men do not interact during that encounter, it has a profound impact on Listwell, who vows to go home and "atone for my past indifference to this ill-starred race, by making such exertions as I shall be able to do, for the speedy emancipation of every slave in the land."[7]

Throughout the account, Douglass often focuses on the white characters' emotions rather than on those of the hero. After Madison recounts his escape to the Listwells, he takes refuge in their home, and Douglass writes, "We pass over the thoughts and feelings, the hopes

> **Argument Three**
> The author's third argument focuses on Madison's interaction with and influence upon white characters: "Douglass most often shows Madison in the presence of white characters, from whose point of view readers see the story."

> **Argument Four**
> This is the final argument: "Throughout the account, Douglass often focuses on the white characters' emotions rather than on those of the hero." Here the author shows how focusing on the white characters' emotions rather than Madison's helps the white readers connect with the story.

and fears, the plans and purposes, that revolved in the mind of Madison."[8] Once Madison is safely in Canada, readers learn little about how he feels, as Douglass focuses instead on Listwell and the "joy and gratification which knew no bounds" he experienced after helping the slave escape.[9] And Madison's final triumph, the mutiny abroad the *Creole*, is recounted entirely by a white character; the hero does not even appear in the scene. Tom Grant's stirring recount shows his admiration of the slave, saying, "I felt myself in the presence of a superior man."[10] Even though Madison seizes control of Grant's own crew, Madison's speech and actions persuade Grant that slavery is wrong.

Ultimately, "The Heroic Slave" is antislavery literature intended for white audiences. By presenting his hero in terms that would appeal to these readers, Douglass hoped to affect readers in the way Madison affected Listwell and Grant. If readers could identify with Madison, they might be willing to speak out against slavery—or to go even further and take action against it.

Conclusion

The conclusion restates the thesis. It claims Douglass wants Madison to appeal to white readers so they will accept the hero and, ultimately, the cause of abolitionism.

Thinking Critically about "The Heroic Slave"

Now it is your turn to assess the critique.
Consider these questions:

1. The author argues that Madison appeals to nineteenth-century white readers. Do you agree? Are there ways in which he might not appeal to these readers?

2. Which argument is the strongest? Which is the weakest? Why? Are there other arguments that might show how Madison appeals to nineteenth-century white readers?

3. Do you agree with the author's conclusion that Douglass was using the work to move white readers to take action against slavery? Why or why not?

Other Approaches

Every type of criticism allows for multiple approaches to the text. The previous critique examines how Douglass presents his hero, Madison Washington, in an appealing way to a nineteenth-century white audience. The following are two other possible approaches to a racial critique of this work, including an examination of how white characters help Madison by listening to him and a discussion of how the story presents both good and bad white characters.

Black Speakers, White Listeners

In "Sympathetic Listening in Frederick Douglass's 'The Heroic Slave' and *My Bondage and My Freedom*," professor and literary critic Marianne Noble argues that the novella shows positive relations between blacks and whites, because white characters listen to what black characters have to say. The character of Listwell, for example, listens well (hence his name) as Madison tells his story. A thesis for a critique based on this argument might be: Douglass shows how positive relationships can develop between races if blacks speak out about their circumstances and whites listen to them.

Good Whites, Bad Whites

In "The Heroic Slave," Douglass presents several types of white characters. There is Listwell, a kind, courageous man who immediately converts to abolitionism; Tom Grant, who eventually acknowledges the injustice of slavery; and the crude, coarse slave traders and owners, who see slaves as nothing more than property. A thesis for a critique analyzing the different white characters in the book might be: In "The Heroic Slave," Douglass demonstrates that white characters can be both slaves' worst enemies and their greatest allies.

Douglass was a skilled orator who captivated—and challenged—his audience.

An Overview of "What to the Slave Is the Fourth of July?"

On July 5, 1852, Douglass delivered a Fourth of July speech at Corinthian Hall in Rochester, New York. Speaking at the request of the Rochester Ladies' Anti-Slavery Society, Douglass used the celebration of the nation's independence to highlight the lack of freedom slaves in the United States experienced. The speech was met with strong applause from the audience of more than 500, and afterward it was published in pamphlet form.[1]

The Story of the Fourth of July

Douglass begins his speech by claiming to be unequal to the great task before him, of speaking on the occasion of the nation's Independence Day. He reminds listeners of the significance of the Fourth of July: it is a day to celebrate the struggle for freedom and the signing of the Declaration of Independence only 76 years earlier. Douglass encourages his audience to hold fast to the "saving principles" of that declaration: "Stand by those principles, be true to them on all occasions, in all places, against all foes, and at whatever cost."[2] Douglass also honors the men who signed the Declaration of Independence, saying they "loved their country better than their own private interests."[3]

Problems in the Present

After speaking of the nation's glorious past, Douglass turns his attention to its present. He reminds his audience the Founding Fathers were not content to let injustices go unchallenged, yet present-day Americans choose to let the injustices of slavery continue. He stresses that George Washington freed his own slaves in his will, yet present-day Americans create new laws to continue to uphold the institution of slavery.

Douglass then asks why he, of all people, has been called upon to speak on the anniversary of the nation's independence. He says he and his people have nothing to do with the nation's freedom because unlike the rest of the country's population,

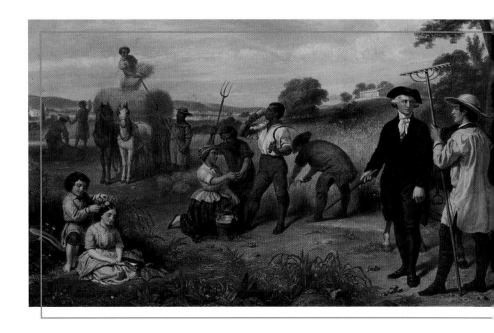

they are not free. He even poses the question of whether his being asked to speak on this day is a form of mockery.

Douglass reminds his audience that George Washington was a slave owner, but he freed his slaves upon his death in his will.

No Need for Argument

Douglass acknowledges that some people think he and other abolitionists spend too much time rebuking and denouncing those who uphold slavery and too little time presenting arguments that explain why the institution should be abolished. But he contends there is nothing to argue. There is no need for him to prove that a slave is a man because the slaveholders themselves have proven that. If slaves were not men, the slaveholders would not make laws for them. After all, animals are not expected to obey laws.

Douglass also says there is no need for him to prove slaves have a right to liberty. The country itself has declared that right in its Declaration of Independence. He also states, "There is not a man beneath the canopy of heaven, that does not know that slavery is wrong for him."[4] He further argues that slavery is not ordained by God, as some have argued, for the institution is inhuman and therefore cannot be divine.

After demonstrating that it is unnecessary to present arguments against slavery, Douglass delivers the famous line, "What, to the American slave, is your 4th of July?"[5] He then answers his own question: it is a day on which slaves are reminded—more than on any other day—of the injustices they suffer.

Denouncing the Slave Trade

As an example of those injustices, Douglass turns to a discussion of the slave trade within the United States. He describes how the US government keeps a squadron, or naval fleet, on the coast of

Africa to prevent Africans from being taken to serve as slaves, and yet the slave trade within the United States' borders flourishes under the title "internal slave trade." Douglass goes on to give a vivid description of that trade. Men and women are raised like pigs and then forced to walk to the slave market, prodded on by the slave driver's whip. When they get to the slave market, they are roughly examined and then sold, often separated from loved ones forever.

In addition to the injustice of the slave market, Douglass addresses the injustice of the Fugitive Slave Law, which makes it legal for slave-hunters to seek runaway slaves in the free North. When captured, a runaway slave has no right to speak in his own defense and is sent back to a life of slavery.

The Church's Part

After criticizing the Fugitive Slave Law in general, Douglass rebukes the nation's Christian churches and their ministers for not speaking out against the act. He says even as ministers enjoy their own religious freedom, they remain silent in the face of a law that takes away the freedom of others. Beyond failing to speak up on behalf

of the slaves, the church actually takes the side
of slaveholders. Douglass points out that some
ministers have said slavery is an institution ordained
by God.

Douglass faults Christian churches not only for
upholding slavery but also for failing to abolish
it. He says if Christians spoke out against slavery,
the cruel institution would be unable to stand.
Continuing his argument against churches in the
United States, Douglass contrasts it with the English
church, which took an active part in that country's
antislavery movement.

Douglass bitterly asserts that both mainstream
US religions and the US political system are
inconsistent: Americans praise themselves for their
dedication to liberty and Christian values, even as
they continue to enslave millions of their fellow
men and women. The United States welcomes
refugees from overseas to its shores, but it viciously
hunts down those who have escaped the bonds of
slavery within its own borders.

Turning to the Constitution

Douglass then turns to the US Constitution,
saying many defenders of slavery claim this

document guarantees Americans the right to keep slaves. If this were the case, Douglass says, then the nation's Founding Fathers were not the honest, heroic men he has proclaimed them to be but rather imposters who only pretended to believe in freedom.

Douglass does not believe this is the case, though. Instead, he argues the Constitution was never meant to support slavery. Furthermore, Douglass holds that the Constitution is by its very nature antislavery.

A Hopeful Conclusion

As he concludes his speech, Douglass reassures his audience he is not without hope for the future of the nation. He trusts slavery will eventually be overthrown. As the countries of the world establish closer relationships, the United States will no longer be able to continue on the path of slavery without interference. Douglass ends his speech by quoting a poem penned by fellow abolitionist William Lloyd Garrison. The poem looks forward with hope to the day when all men and women are free and treated as equals—a goal that can be achieved "whate'er the peril or the cost."[6]

Douglass made his audience question the celebration of Independence Day while slaves were denied basic freedom.

8

How to Apply Reader-Response Criticism to "What to the Slave Is the Fourth of July?"

No. 2

What Is Reader-Response Criticism?

As its name implies, reader-response criticism deals with how a reader (or a listener, in the case of a speech) responds to a work. Reader-response critics believe the meaning of a text lies in how a reader interprets that text. Critics may analyze their own responses to a work. Or they may choose to focus on how the average reader or a specific type of reader would interpret the text.

Applying Reader-Response Criticism to "What to the Slave Is the Fourth of July?"

Although the occasion for his speech was the celebration of the United States' independence, many of those gathered to hear Douglass on July 5, 1852, probably expected he would speak

Thesis Statement

The author presents the thesis statement at the end of the first paragraph: "As they listened to Douglass's speech, even the staunchest abolitionists were made to feel like hypocrites." The author examines how audience members come to recognize their own hypocrisy in claiming to oppose slavery but allowing it to continue.

Argument One

This is the first argument: "Douglass makes it clear that audience members are hypocritical for even celebrating the Fourth of July." The author examines why audience members should feel like hypocrites for celebrating Independence Day.

about slavery. After all, he was a well-known abolitionist, speaking at a meeting of the Rochester Ladies' Anti-Slavery Society. And many of those in the audience were like-minded abolitionists. But Douglass's speech went further than anyone had expected. As they listened to Douglass's speech, even the staunchest abolitionists were made to feel like hypocrites.

Douglass makes it clear that audience members are hypocritical for even celebrating the Fourth of July. The day is a celebration of freedom, but millions of people in the country are denied freedom and held in slavery. As Douglass points out, "This Fourth [of] July is *yours*, not *mine*. *You* may rejoice, *I* must mourn."[1] Because of this, he wonders if he was asked to speak on this particular day as a form of mockery. For Douglass, as for all slaves, the Fourth of July is one more reminder that the freedoms enjoyed by whites are withheld from them. Douglass makes listeners feel the full force of their hypocrisy, saying that while they claim to be opposed to slavery, they still celebrate this day of independence: "Your celebration is a sham; . . . your shouts of liberty and equality, hollow mockery; your prayers and hymns, your sermons and thanksgivings, . . . are, to [the slave], mere bombast, fraud, deception, impiety, and hypocrisy."[2]

<u>Douglass's focus on the Founding Fathers' courageous fight for freedom also leads audience members to see the hypocrisy of their own complacency in the face of slavery.</u> Douglass lauds the men who signed the Declaration of Independence. Although they were "peace men," they "preferred revolution to peaceful submission to bondage."[3] Of course, there were those who were willing to remain in bondage to the British government. Douglass contends that such people hated change, "no matter

> **Argument Two**
> The author presents the second argument: "Douglass's focus on the Founding Fathers' courageous fight for freedom also leads audience members to see the hypocrisy of their own complacency in the face of slavery." In this paragraph, the author looks at the difference between the Founding Fathers' revolutionary attitude and the complacency of his audience members.

how great the good to be attained, or the wrong to be redressed by it."[4] As Douglass upholds the Founding Fathers above those who refused to take action, audience members once again feel their own hypocrisy. If they are unwilling to take action against slavery and instead sit by as men and women continue to be held in bondage, they are no better than the cowards who refused to participate in the United States' fight for freedom.

Douglass's focus on the internal slave trade and the Fugitive Slave Law serves to further arouse his listeners' feelings of hypocrisy. Douglass points out that the internal slave trade—the trade of slaves between states—continued "in one-half of this confederacy" without condemnation.[5] Even if his listeners did not participate in the slave trade or did not live in states where it was conducted, they, as Americans, were responsible for its continuation because their national government allowed the trade to continue. Similarly, the Fugitive Slave Law implicated all Americans in the

> **Argument Three**
>
> The author next focuses on how Douglass's discussion of the internal slave trade and the Fugitive Slave Law continues to show the listeners' hypocrisy. The third argument is: "Douglass's focus on the internal slave trade and the Fugitive Slave Law serves to further arouse his listeners' feelings of hypocrisy."

institution of slavery. The law required everyone—
from the North or South—to turn over runaway
slaves, who would then be returned to slavery.
Douglass reminds listeners that "your President,
your Secretary of State, your *lords*, *nobles*, and
ecclesiastics, enforce, as a duty you owe to your
free and glorious country, and to your God," that
they participate in the "hellish sport" of slave-
hunting.[6] Such a requirement makes everyone a
participant in slavery.

Finally, listeners are made to
feel like hypocrites for belonging
to churches that claim to be
Christian but fail to demonstrate
Christian love. He accuses the
US church of esteeming "psalm-
singing above right doing" and
"solemn meetings above practical
righteousness."[7] In fact, he says,
the church has gone so far as
to say the Bible allows—and even condones—
slavery. Douglass says his accusations are true of
"the popular church, and the popular worship of
our land and nation."[8] In other words, it is true of
the churches at which his listeners worship. Thus,

> **Argument Four**
> The final argument is: "Finally,
> listeners are made to feel
> like hypocrites for belonging
> to churches that claim to
> be Christian but fail to
> demonstrate Christian love."
> In this paragraph, the author
> looks at the hypocrisy of the
> Christian church in the United
> States, to which many of the
> listeners belonged.

Conclusion

The conclusion restates the thesis and summarizes the arguments that the author made. It highlights Douglass's hope that one day, such hypocrisy—along with slavery—would come to an end.

they are participants in their churches' hypocrisy.

Even as they celebrated the freedoms won for them on the Fourth of July 76 years earlier, audience members listening to Douglass's speech couldn't help but be struck by their own hypocrisy. In celebrating Independence Day, in allowing the internal slave trade and the Fugitive Slave Law to continue, and in supporting the US church, listeners were upholding the institution of slavery, even as they claimed to oppose it. Yet despite their participation in such "national inconsistencies," Douglass held out hope that such hypocrisy would come to an end—and with it, slavery would end, too.[9]

Thinking Critically about "What to the Slave Is the Fourth of July?"

Now it is your turn to assess the critique. Consider these questions:

1. The author contends that white abolitionist listeners feel like hypocrites as a result of Douglass's speech. Do you agree with the author's thesis? Why or why not?

2. Which of the author's arguments is the strongest? Which is the weakest? Why?

3. Are there other ways for listeners to respond to this speech? Could they feel guilty, hopeful, or angry, for example? What arguments from the text support such responses?

Other Approaches

This essay provides one example of how reader-response criticism can be applied to Douglass's speech. Because each reader (or listener) is different, there are many ways this speech could be interpreted. The following are two alternative approaches. One approach discusses how Douglass's audience may have found his speech quite surprising on that Independence Day. Another approach argues that Douglass's audience may have interpreted his speech as a call to revolutionary action against slavery.

A Surprising Fourth of July Oration

Some listeners may find Douglass's Fourth of July speech surprising because it does not meet their expectations for a speech in celebration of the nation's independence. Instead of praising the United States, as most Independence Day speakers tend to do, Douglass takes the opposite approach and criticizes the nation. A thesis statement for a critique that takes this perspective could be: Listeners' expectations for Douglass's Fourth of July speech are turned upside down as he criticizes the country's celebration of independence.

A Call to Action

Although Douglass generally favored peaceful resistance to slavery, some might see in his Fourth of July speech a call to take decisive action against the institution. Some listeners might interpret Douglass's description of the United States' Founding Fathers—men of peace who yet "preferred revolution to peaceful submission to bondage"—as a call to begin a revolution against slavery.[10] A thesis in support of this argument might be: As Douglass describes the revolutionary actions of the Founding Fathers, listeners feel compelled to take similar action to put an end to slavery.

Douglass delivered his "Lessons of the Hour" speech in 1894, one year before his death.

9

An Overview of
"Lessons of the Hour"

Although the ratification of the Thirteenth
Amendment in 1865 brought slavery to an end,
Southern whites' treatment of African Americans
had steadily deteriorated after the end of
Reconstruction, which spanned from the end of the
Civil War to 1877. In fact, the country frequently
spoke of its "Negro problem," and white mobs
regularly carried out lynchings of free Southern
blacks.[1]

Douglass addressed these issues in his last
great speech, "Lessons of the Hour," which he
delivered on January 9, 1894. According to the *Post*
newspaper, Douglass gave the speech "with a fire
which showed that the vigor of his youth had not
forsaken him."[2]

The Purpose

Douglass begins his speech by saying his purpose is to present a black man's view of the current state of affairs between blacks and whites in the South. He refers to the "so-called, but miscalled, Negro problem" as a subject in urgent need of address.[3] He contends that the problem and its solution involve all Americans, for the "sport of mob violence and murder" threatens to overthrow the rule of law.[4]

The Southern mob, Douglass says, has seemingly given itself the right to prosecute and punish any black man accused of raping a white woman. The accused is given no opportunity to defend himself and has no right to a fair trial. He is instead immediately seized and killed by the mob. Despite the injustice of the situation, the majority of the people in the South approve of the mob's actions, and the majority of whites in the North acquiesce to the practice.

Douglass agrees that assaulting a woman is the most horrid crime imaginable. But, he says, the charge of rape is being brought not against an individual but against the entire Negro race, making every black man an object of suspicion. Douglass does not deny that some Negroes may commit this crime, but he does "utterly deny that they are any more addicted to the commission of that crime than is true of any other variety of the human family."[5] Thus, his speech is not in defense of those who commit the crime, but in defense of the race.

Making the Case

Douglass goes on to confidently assert he will plead not guilty on behalf of the black race and will submit a case that upholds that plea. He first argues that members of a mob should not be relied on as witnesses, especially when that same mob condemns and kills the accused. He also questions the character of Southern white men and defends the character of black men.

Douglass realizes some Northerners believe the charges against these black men must be true, thinking that normal men would not make up such charges simply to have an excuse to hang and kill others. But, Douglass says, these Northerners fail to take into account the Southern mob has been raised in the midst of a slaveholding society and therefore has no respect for life. As he says, "A dead Negro is with them a common jest."[6]

Criticism of World's Columbian Exposition

Douglass next criticizes the World's Columbian Exposition, held in Chicago, for discriminating against the Negro. Douglass himself was a commissioner at this event, representing Haiti. In his speech, he states that although people from around the world were represented, the educated American Negro was left out. Such exclusions simply serve to justify the lynchers, Douglass says.

Negro Suffrage

Douglass then turns his attention to the subject of Negro suffrage. He says many people blame the troubles in the South on the fact that blacks have been given the right to vote. Thus, many want to require blacks to prove their education in order to vote.

However, Douglass maintains black suffrage has not caused trouble in the South. Rather, the trouble occurs when Southern whites lawlessly keep blacks from exercising their right to vote. Douglass condemns those who have considered going so far as to take that right away from blacks.

Colonization

Douglass states that some people have proposed resettling blacks in an African colony or elsewhere as a solution to the Negro problem. Douglass denounces the scheme. Africa is not the black people's native land: "The native land of the American Negro is America. His bones, his muscles, his sinews, are all American."[7]

Douglass also discusses how, looking at the lot of the Negro in the South, some people have said freedom has been bad for black people. Although Douglass says such an assertion is mostly false, he admits it is partly true. In some ways and in some places, he says, black men and women are more miserable now than they were under slavery. But the cause of their misery is not freedom. Instead, the cause is the new economic system of the South, which is almost equivalent to a new form of slavery.

The "Negro Problem"

Douglass now begins to discuss the "Negro problem." He rejects this name for the problem, because it places blame solely on black Americans and presents the entire race as a "problem." No matter what name the issue is called, though, the important thing is figuring out how to solve it. And unless it is solved, Douglass says, the nation may experience divine punishment for its wrongs. The problem cannot be solved, Douglass says, by keeping Negroes in poverty or repealing their right to vote. Instead, it will be solved by overcoming prejudices, learning kindness, and paying fair wages. It will be solved by ceasing to ignore the Constitution and justice.

Over the years, Negro rights have been questioned on many occasions, Douglass says. People once wondered whether Negroes had the right to baptism, marriage, citizenship, or education. All these questions have been answered, Douglass says. Negroes have become doctors and lawyers, have served on battlefields, and have excelled "in every useful calling."[8] Yet they are still called "'a problem;' 'a tremendous problem;' a mountain of difficulty; a constant source of apprehension; a disturbing force, threatening destruction to the holiest and best interests of society."[9]

In conclusion, Douglass calls upon the people of the United States to remember the principles upon which their nation was founded. If Americans

acknowledge the rights of all people—not just some—their problems will be solved, and their nation will "stand and flourish forever."[10]

Douglass urges Americans— whites and blacks alike—to resolve the "problem" by voting and upholding the Constitution.

Douglass advocates for African Americans, presenting a case like a lawyer against the "Negro problem."

How to Apply Rhetorical Criticism to "Lessons of the Hour"

What Is Rhetorical Criticism?

Rhetoric refers to the art of speaking or writing persuasively. It has been a topic of study for more than 2,000 years, since the time of the ancient Greeks. Modern rhetorical criticism analyzes how a speaker or writer uses language to communicate with or influence an audience. In conducting rhetorical analysis, a critic may consider several questions: What is the purpose of the work being analyzed? What historical situation or circumstance does it address? Who is the intended audience? How does the speaker structure his or her arguments? Does the speaker appeal to emotion or to reason? Answering such questions can help the critic better understand a speaker's rhetorical method and the effect it achieves.

Applying Rhetorical Criticism to "Lessons of the Hour"

By the late nineteenth century, the United States found itself dealing with a "Negro problem," a name coined by whites—and even used by some blacks—in both the South and the North.[1] But Douglass believed the problem was misnamed, as he asserts in his last great speech, "Lessons of the Hour." Throughout the speech, Douglass relies on strong language and biting irony, along with appeals to emotion and logic, to prove the so-called Negro problem has little to do with the Negro and more to do with the nation.

Douglass's characteristically strong language demonstrates the problem is with white attitudes and actions rather than with Negroes. Douglass condemns the Southern mob in the harshest terms possible, comparing it to "the lowest and

Thesis Statement

The thesis is stated at the end of this paragraph: "Throughout the speech, Douglass relies on strong language and biting irony, along with appeals to emotion and logic, to prove the so-called Negro problem has little to do with the Negro and more to do with the nation." The rest of the critique proves the thesis.

Argument One

The author begins with Douglass's use of harsh criticism: "Douglass's characteristically strong language demonstrates the problem is with white attitudes and actions rather than with Negroes."

most disgusting birds and beasts, such as buzzards, vultures, and hyenas."[2] Douglass further claims that Southern men, having been raised in a slaveholding culture, are not like other men: their nature has been "corrupted and perverted by long abuse of irresponsible power," and they do not have "any such respect for human life as is common to other men."[3] Douglass does not reserve his scathing words for the people of the South, though. He also condemns the organizers of the World's Columbian Exposition, held in the Northern city of Chicago, for failing to include educated American blacks. Douglass says such an exclusion in a Northern event may seem harmless, but it is no better than the Southern lynchers' actions: "It says to the lynchers and mobocrats of the South, go on in your hellish work of Negro persecution. What you do to their bodies, we do to their souls."[4]

In this speech, as in many of his others, Douglass calls upon irony and sarcasm for his harshest criticisms. He begins by noting the barbarity against Negroes is being carried out by the "so-called enlightened and

> **Argument Two**
> This is the second argument: "In this speech, as in many of his others, Douglass calls upon irony and sarcasm for his harshest criticisms." The paragraph gives examples of how Douglass uses irony and sarcasm to make his point.

Christian people of the South."[5] Douglass criticizes not just the mob; he also sarcastically notes the "better classes of the Southern States" approve the mob's actions.[6] Douglass points out the irony that black men are being killed for supposedly raping white women, when the system of slavery "was a system of legalized outrage upon the black women of the South, and no white man was ever shot, burned, or hanged" for raping a black woman.[7] Ultimately, Douglass finds the "Negro problem" ironic, since the Negro is "neither a Lyncher, a Mobocrat, or an Anarchist" like his accusers.[8]

Using more than just irony, Douglass appeals to his listeners' sympathy as well by showing that Negroes are the victims of the "Negro problem," not the cause. He points out the country's 8 million black people are "smarting under terrible wrongs" as they are "denied the exercise of the commonest rights of humanity."[9] Douglass then describes a lynching in direct, powerful language that elicits the scene in his listeners' minds. The accused, he says, "is bound with cords,

Argument Three

The third argument focuses on Douglass's use of emotional appeal: "Using more than just irony, Douglass appeals to his listeners' sympathy as well by showing that Negroes are the victims of the 'Negro problem,' not the cause."

. . . tortured . . . and then whether innocent or guilty, he is shot, hanged, stabbed, or burned to death amid the wild shouts of the mob."[10] Even blacks who are not lynched suffer from the system, as their white friends, both North and South, now regard all black men with "averted eyes, increasing hate and dark suspicion."[11]

Ultimately, Douglass's case that the problem is national rather than Negro relies most heavily on appeals to logic. Like a lawyer, Douglass lays out a case to prove Negroes as a race are not guilty of the crime of which they are accused. He first defends the character of the black man. He points out that black slaves were left alone with their slave owners' wives, sisters, and children during the Civil War, but "there was never a single instance of such crime reported or charged against [them]."[12] It is illogical to believe the Negro character has suddenly changed and now they have begun to rape white women when they have less opportunity than they previously had. Douglass goes on to discuss Negro suffrage,

> **Argument Four**
>
> In the final argument, the author shows how Douglass relies on logic to make his point: "Ultimately, Douglass's case that the problem is national rather than Negro relies most heavily on appeals to logic." The paragraph provides examples of Douglass's logical appeals.

which some have also blamed as a cause of the "Negro problem." To Douglass, such a contention is an "outrage upon common sense and common fairness."[13] Those who propose it cannot show any "oppressive and hurtful measure has been imposed upon the country by Negro voters."[14] Lastly, Douglass uses logic to attack the "false reasoners" who assert that emancipation is the cause of the "Negro problem."[15] He shows it is not freedom that has harmed blacks but rather the new Southern economic system that makes blacks beholden to their white landlords.

Conclusion
The conclusion restates the thesis. It focuses on why Douglass thought the "Negro problem" was misnamed and explains his hope for the entire nation to find a solution to it.

Douglass's harsh words, emotional appeals, and logical arguments are aimed at persuading his audience that the country does not have a "Negro problem." Indeed, the name "makes the Negro responsible and not the nation."[16] Yet, it is a national problem, as Douglass proves, and it will take the whole nation and all its virtue to solve it.

Thinking Critically about "Lessons of the Hour"

Now it is your turn to assess the critique. Consider these questions:

1. The author argues that Douglass uses strong language, biting irony, emotion, and logic to persuade his listeners. Which of Douglass's methods do you think is most effective? Which is least effective? Why?

2. Does Douglass use any other rhetorical devices in his speech? Give examples.

3. What other ideas might Douglass's rhetoric persuade listeners to believe? Do you think his rhetoric is likely to lead his listeners to take action?

Other Approaches

The critique you have just read is one way to apply rhetorical criticism to "Lessons of the Hour." It examines how Douglass uses harsh language, irony, and appeals to logic and emotion to prove the "Negro problem" was really a problem before the entire nation. The following are two other possible approaches. One discusses how Douglass's speech differed from that of his contemporary orators'. Another approach examines Douglass's limited, but vivid, use of imagery.

A Different Kind of Orator

According to US historian John Blassingame, "The typical nineteenth-century oration was long, ponderous, and filled with stilted grammar, classical allusions, strings of rhetorical questions, Latin phrases, protracted perorations [long conclusions], and rich imagery."[17] Douglass's speeches, in contrast, were "refreshingly simple."[18] A thesis for a critique examining this topic might be this: While other nineteenth-century orators often delivered long, difficult speeches, Douglass spoke in a relatively simpler, more direct style that better appealed to his audience.

Proper Use of Imagery

Writers and orators alike call upon imagery to paint vivid scenes in the minds of their readers and listeners, respectively. According to Longinus, an ancient Greek rhetorical critic, in his book *On the Sublime*, "The dignity, grandeur, and energy of a style largely depend on a proper employment of images."[19] Specifically referring to the use of imagery in oration, Longinus states, "when it is mingled with the practical, argumentative parts of an oration, it does not merely convince the hearer, but enthralls him."[20]

In "Lessons of the Hour," Douglass uses imagery sparingly, more often using practical, argumentative language. He reserves imagery mostly to describe the violence and horror of lynching, which creates a powerful impact that stirs his audience's emotions. A thesis statement for a critique examining how Douglass uses imagery might be the following: In his largely argumentative speech "Lessons of the Hour," Douglass uses imagery sparingly to create a violent, emotional picture of lynching.

You Critique It

Now that you have learned about different critical theories and how to apply them to different works, are you ready to perform your own critique? You have read that this type of evaluation can help you look at books, speeches, and essays in new ways and make you pay attention to certain issues you may not have otherwise recognized. So, why not use one of the critical theories profiled in this book to consider a fresh take on your favorite work?

First, choose a theory and the work you want to analyze. Remember that the theory is a springboard for asking questions about the work.

Next, write a specific question that relates to the theory you have selected. Then you can form your thesis, which should provide the answer to that question. Your thesis is the most important part of your critique and offers an argument about the work based on the tenets, or beliefs, of the theory you are applying. Recall that the thesis statement typically appears at the very end of the introductory paragraph of your essay. It is usually only one sentence long.

After you have written your thesis, find evidence to back it up. Good places to start are in the work itself or in journals or articles that discuss what other people have said about it. If you are critiquing a speech, you may also want to read about the speaker's life so you can get a sense of what factors may have affected the creation of the speech. This can be especially useful if working within historical or biographical criticism.

Depending on which theory you are applying, you can often find evidence in the work's language, structure, or historical context. You should also explore parts of the work that seem to disprove your thesis and create an argument against them. As you do this, you might want to address what other critics have written about the work. Their quotes may help support your claim.

Before you start analyzing a work, think about the different arguments made in this book. Reflect on how evidence supporting the thesis was presented. Did you find that some of the techniques used to back up the arguments were more convincing than others? Try these methods as you prove your thesis in your own critique.

When you are finished writing your critique, read it over carefully. Is your thesis statement understandable? Do the supporting arguments flow logically, with the topic of each paragraph clearly stated? Can you add any information that would present your readers with a stronger argument in favor of your thesis? Were you able to use quotes from the work, as well as from other critics, to enhance your ideas?

Did you see the work in a new light?

Timeline

1818 In February, Frederick Douglass is born in Tuckahoe, Maryland, to a slave mother and white father.

1826 Douglass is sent to Baltimore to serve Hugh and Sophia Auld.

1834 Douglass is sent to Edward Covey, a notorious "slave breaker," who frequently beats him.

1835 Douglass is hired out to work for William Freeland and secretly teaches other slaves to read.

1836 Douglass formulates a plan to escape, but his plan is discovered and he is sent back to Hugh and Sophia Auld.

1838 Douglass escapes to New York City on September 3; on September 15, Douglass marries Anna Murray, and the two move to New Bedford, Massachusetts.

1860 Douglass's youngest daughter dies on March 13, prompting his return to the United States.

1863 Douglass recruits black soldiers for the Fifty-fourth Massachusetts Volunteers and meets with President Abraham Lincoln to discuss black service in the armed forces.

1871 Douglass is appointed secretary of the Santo Domingo Commission.

1874 In March, Douglass becomes president of the Freedman's Savings and Trust Company in Washington DC, which fails four months later.

1877 Douglass becomes marshal of the District of Columbia.

1881 Douglass becomes recorder of deeds for the District of Columbia and publishes his final autobiography, *The Life and Times of Frederick Douglass*.

1882 Douglass's wife Anna dies of a stroke on August 4.

1884 On January 24, Douglass marries Helen Pitts, a white woman, stirring up controversy among his family as well as the public.

1889 Douglass moves to Haiti in October to serve as US minister there.

1841 Douglass speaks at a meeting of the Massachusetts Anti-Slavery Society on August 16 and is afterward hired as a speaker for the society.

1845 *Narrative of the Life of Frederick Douglass, An American Slave, Written by Himself* is published, and Douglass leaves for a speaking tour in Great Britain.

1847 Douglass returns to the United States as a free man; Douglass begins publishing the antislavery newspaper *North Star* in Rochester, New York.

1852 Douglass's only work of fiction, "The Heroic Slave," is published; Douglass delivers a Fourth of July speech in Rochester, New York.

1855 *My Bondage and My Freedom*, Douglass's second autobiography, is published.

1859 Douglass arrives in Britain for a speaking tour after fleeing the United States for fear of being implicated in John Brown's raid on Harpers Ferry.

1893 At the World's Columbian Exposition, Douglass serves as commissioner of the Republic of Haiti pavilion.

1894 Douglass delivers his "Lessons of the Hour" speech on January 9.

1895 Douglass dies of a heart attack on February 20.

Glossary

abolitionist

A person working in support of the movement to end slavery.

acquiescence

The act of accepting or agreeing with something.

complacency

A feeling of satisfaction with oneself without an awareness of pending danger or problems.

emancipation

The act of being freed from slavery.

fetters

Chains or shackles.

hypocrisy

The act of pretending to be what one is not.

implicate

To form a connection that suggests a person is guilty of a crime.

irony

The use of words to express the opposite of their actual meaning.

lynch
> To put to death (often by hanging) without a lawful trial.

novella
> A work of fiction that is longer than a short story but shorter than a novel.

orator
> A person who makes public speeches.

repeal
> To officially cancel or reverse a law.

stereotype
> A simplified, often prejudiced, view of what members of a certain group look like, how they act, or what they believe.

suffrage
> The right to vote.

Bibliography of Works and Criticism

Important Works

"I Have Come to Tell You Something about Slavery,"
1841

Narrative of the Life of Frederick Douglass, 1845

"American Slavery, American Religion, and the Free
Church of Scotland," 1846

"What to the American Slave is the Fourth of July?,"
1852

"The Heroic Slave," 1852

My Bondage and My Freedom, 1855

"The Dred Scot Decision," 1857

"Men of Color, To Arms!," 1863

"What the Black Man Wants," 1865

"Let the Negro Alone," 1869

"At Last, at Last, the Black Man Has a Future," 1870

"Oration on the Occasion of the Dedication of the
Lincoln Monument," 1876

Life and Times of Frederick Douglass, 1881, 1892

"Self-Made Men," 1893

"Lessons of the Hour," 1894

Critical Discussions

Colaiaco, James A. *Frederick Douglass and the Fourth of July*. New York: Palgrave Macmillan, 2006. Print.

Fulkerson, Gerald. "Frederick Douglass." *African-American Orators: A Bio-Critical Sourcebook*. Ed. Richard W. Leeman. Westport, CT: Greenwood, 1996. Print.

Ring, Betty J. "'Painting by Numbers': Figuring Frederick Douglass." *The Discourse of Slavery: Aphra Behn to Toni Morrison*. Ed. Carl Plasa and Betty J. Ring. New York: Routledge, 1994. Print.

Sisco, Lisa. "'Writing in the Spaces Left': Literacy as a Process of Becoming in the Narratives of Frederick Douglass." *ATQ* 9, no. 3. 1995. Print.

Sundquist, Eric J., ed. *Frederick Douglass: New Literary and Historical Essays*. Cambridge, MA: Cambridge UP, 1990. Print.

Sundquist, Eric J., ed. *To Wake the Nations: Race in the Making of American Literature*. Cambridge, MA: Harvard UP, 1993. Print.

Resources

Selected Bibliography

Douglass, Frederick. "The Heroic Slave." *Electronic Text Center*. University of Virginia Library, n.d. Web. 15 July 2012.

Douglass, Frederick. "Lessons of the Hour." *Antislavery Literature*. Antislavery Literature Project, n.d. Web. 15 July 2012.

Douglass, Frederick. *The Narrative of the Life of Frederick Douglass, an American Slave, Written by Himself*. Ed. George Stade. New York: Barnes & Noble, 2003. Print.

McFeely, William S. *Frederick Douglass*. New York: Norton, 1991. Print.

Further Readings

Adler, David A. *Frederick Douglass: A Noble Life*. New York: Holiday, 2010.

McKivigan, John R., ed. *Frederick Douglass*. San Diego: Greenhaven, 2004. Print.

Web Links

To learn more about critiquing the works of Frederick Douglass, visit ABDO Publishing Company online at **www.abdopublishing.com**. Web sites about the works of Frederick Douglass are featured on our Book Links page. These links are routinely monitored and updated to provide the most current information available.

For More Information

Frederick Douglass National Historic Site
1411 W Street SE, Washington, DC 20020
www.nps.gov/frdo/index.htm

The Frederick Douglass National Historic site is located at Douglass's former home.

Frederick Douglass Resource Center
36 King Street, Rochester, NY 14608
585-325-9190
www.frederickdouglassrc.com/default.asp

The center is dedicated to educating visitors about the life and legacy of Frederick Douglass and other abolitionists.

Source Notes

Chapter 1. Introduction to Critiques
None.

Chapter 2. A Closer Look at Frederick Douglass
None.

Chapter 3. An Overview of *Narrative of the Life of Frederick Douglass*
    1. William S. McFeely. *Frederick Douglass*. New York: Norton, 1991. Print. 117.
    2. Frederick Douglass. *The Narrative of the Life of Frederick Douglass, an American Slave, Written by Himself*. Ed. George Stade. New York: Barnes & Noble, 2003. Print. 17.
    3. Ibid.39.
    4. Ibid. 49.
    5. Ibid. 58.
    6. Ibid. 62–63.
    7. Ibid. 63.
    8. Ibid. 99.

Chapter 4. How to Apply Moralist Criticism to *Narrative of the Life of Frederick Douglass*
    1. Frederick Douglass. *The Narrative of the Life of Frederick Douglass, an American Slave, Written by Himself*. Ed. George Stade. New York: Barnes & Noble, 2003. Print. 87.
    2. Ibid. 25–26.
    3. Ibid. 46.
    4. Ibid. 62–63.
    5. Ibid. 41.
    6. Ibid.
    7. Ibid. 87.
    8. Ibid. 17.
    9. Ibid. 49–50.
    10. Ibid. 63.
    11. Ibid. 69.
    12. Ibid.

Chapter 5. An Overview of "The Heroic Slave"

1. Frederick Douglass. "The Heroic Slave." *Electronic Text Center*. University of Virginia Library, n.d. Web. 15 July 2012. 174.
2. Ibid. 176.
3. Ibid. 176.
4. Ibid. 187.
5. Ibid. 220.
6. Ibid. 234–35.
7. Ibid. 238.

Chapter 6. How to Apply Racial Criticism to "The Heroic Slave"

1. Richard Yarborough. "Race, Violence, and Manhood." *Frederick Douglass: New Literary and Historical Essays*. Ed. Eric J. Sundquist. Cambridge, MA: Cambridge UP, 1990. Print. 173.
2. Frederick Douglass. "The Heroic Slave." *Electronic Text Center*. University of Virginia Library, n.d. Web. 15 July 2012. 179.
3. Ibid.
4. Ibid. 180.
5. Ibid. 190.
6. Ibid.
7. Ibid. 182.
8. Ibid. 203.
9. Ibid. 204.
10. Ibid. 237.

Chapter 7. An Overview of "What to the Slave Is the Fourth of July?"

1. Frederick Douglass. "What to the Slave is the Fourth of July?" *The Frederick Douglass Papers Series One: Speeches, Debates, and Interviews*. Vol. 2. Ed. John W. Blassingame. New Haven, CT: Yale UP, 1982. Print. 359.
2. Frederick Douglass. "What to the Slave is the Fourth of July?" *University of Rochester Frederick Douglass Project*. University of Rochester Library Department of Rare Books, Special Collections and Preservation, n.d. Web. 15 July 2012. 9.

3. Ibid. 10.

4. Ibid. 19.

5. Ibid. 20.

6. Ibid. 39.

Chapter 8. How to Apply Reader-Response Criticism to "What to the Slave Is the Fourth of July?"

1. Frederick Douglass. "What to the Slave is the Fourth of July?" *University of Rochester Frederick Douglass Project*. University of Rochester Library Department of Rare Books, Special Collections and Preservation, n.d. Web. 15 July 2012. 15.

2. Ibid. 20.

3. Ibid. 10.

4. Ibid. 8.

5. Ibid. 21.

6. Ibid. 25.

7. Ibid. 28.

8. Ibid. 29.

9. Ibid. 34.

10. Ibid. 10.

Chapter 9. An Overview of "Lessons of the Hour"

1. Frederick Douglass. "Lessons of the Hour." *Antislavery Literature*. Antislavery Literature Project, n.d. Web. 15 July 2012. 4.

2. John W. Blassingame, and John R. McKivigan, eds. *The Frederick Douglass Papers Series One: Speeches, Debates, and Interviews*. Vol. 5. New Haven, CT: Yale UP, 1992. Print. 576.

3. Frederick Douglass. "Lessons of the Hour." *Antislavery Literature*. Antislavery Literature Project, n.d. Web. 15 July 2012. 3.

4. Ibid. 4.

5. Ibid. 8.

6. Ibid. 18.

7. Ibid. 26.

8. Ibid. 36.

9. Ibid.

10. Ibid. 70.

Chapter 10. How to Apply Rhetorical Criticism to "Lessons of the Hour"

1. Frederick Douglass. "Lessons of the Hour." *Antislavery Literature*. Antislavery Literature Project, n.d. Web. 15 July 2012. 26.

2. Ibid. 5.

3. Ibid. 17.

4. Ibid. 20.

5. Ibid. 5.

6. Ibid. 6.

7. Ibid. 16.

8. Ibid. 31.

9. Ibid. 4.

10. Ibid. 5.

11. Ibid. 15.

12. Ibid. 11.

13. Ibid. 22.

14. Ibid.

15. Ibid. 28.

16. Ibid. 30.

17. John W. Blassingame, ed. *The Frederick Douglass Papers Series One: Speeches, Debates, and Interviews*. Vol. 1. New Haven, CT: Yale UP, 1979. Print. xxxv.

18. Ibid.

19. Longinus. "On the Sublime." *The Project Gutenberg EBook of On the Sublime, by Longinus*. Project Gutenberg, 10 March 2006. Web. 15 July 2012.

20. Ibid.

Index

About the Author

Valerie Bodden is a freelance author and editor. She has written more than 100 children's nonfiction books. Her books have received positive reviews from *School Library Journal*, *Booklist*, *Children's Literature*, *ForeWord Magazine*, *Horn Book Guide*, *VOYA*, and *Library Media Connection*. Valerie lives in Wisconsin with her husband and their four children.

Photo Credits

Library of Congress, cover, 3, 22; North Wind Picture Archives, 12, 48, 60, 98, 99; Carol M. Highsmith Archive/Library of Congress, 19; Henry Prentiss/Library of Congress, 29; American School/Getty Images, 32; Roger Smith/Library of Congress, 37; William A. Stephens/Library of Congress, 42; AP Images, 50; Detroit Publishing Company/Library of Congress, 54; Junius Brutus Stearns/Library of Congress, 63; J.M. Munyon/Library of Congress, 68; Getty Images, 78, 86; A. W. M'Callum/Library of Congress, 85